When?

A DRAGON Question Book™

By Kathie Billingslea Smith
Illustrated by Robert S. Storms

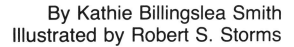

A DRAGON BOOK

GRANADA

When do snake

As your feet grow bigger, your shoes become too small and too tight for you. When that happens, you take off the smaller shoes and get bigger ones that will fit you better.

The same thing happens with snakes and their skins. As a snake grows, its skin gets too small and tight. So the snake grows a new skin and *sheds*, or gets rid of, its old skin.

Snakes shed their skins three or four times a year. Younger snakes shed their skins more often because they grow faster than older snakes.

shed their skins?

BOA
CONSTRICTOR
· UNITED ZOO ·

If you want to see a snake close up, go to the zoo in your town or city. You can look at even poisonous snakes there without being in danger, because the snakes are in glass cages. You may even see a snake that is shedding its skin!

When does a rainbo

Sometimes near the end of a rainstorm, the sun shines out from behind the clouds. And — just like magic — beautiful bands of colour arch across the sky. It's a rainbow!

A rainbow forms when sunlight shines through drops of water in the air. The drops of water split the sunlight into different colours.

orm in the sky?

This can happen in other places too. Rainbows can be found in oil spots on wet roads. Pieces of glass and mirrors and even soap bubbles can split sunlight into rainbow colours, too.

The colours of a rainbow always appear in the same order — red, orange, yellow, green, blue, indigo, and violet. To remember this, just think of the name Roy G. Biv. Each letter of that name stands for a colour in the rainbow!

Triceratops

Diplodocus

The first dinosaurs roamed the earth about 200 million years ago! They lived in the same places we live today, but the land looked different then. It was flat with all kinds of unusual trees and plants. There were ginkgos, swamp cypress, ferns, tree ferns, and horsetails.

Tyrannosaurus Rex

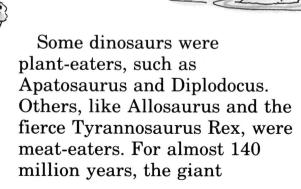

Some dinosaurs were plant-eaters, such as Apatosaurus and Diplodocus. Others, like Allosaurus and the fierce Tyrannosaurus Rex, were meat-eaters. For almost 140 million years, the giant

dinosaurs live?

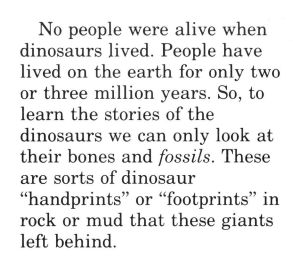

Pteranodon

dinosaurs ruled the land. But slowly the weather got colder and colder and dinosaurs and many other animals and plants began to die out. Only those able to keep warm in the cold lived on.

No people were alive when dinosaurs lived. People have lived on the earth for only two or three million years. So, to learn the stories of the dinosaurs we can only look at their bones and *fossils*. These are sorts of dinosaur "handprints" or "footprints" in rock or mud that these giants left behind.

Fossils

When will the baby

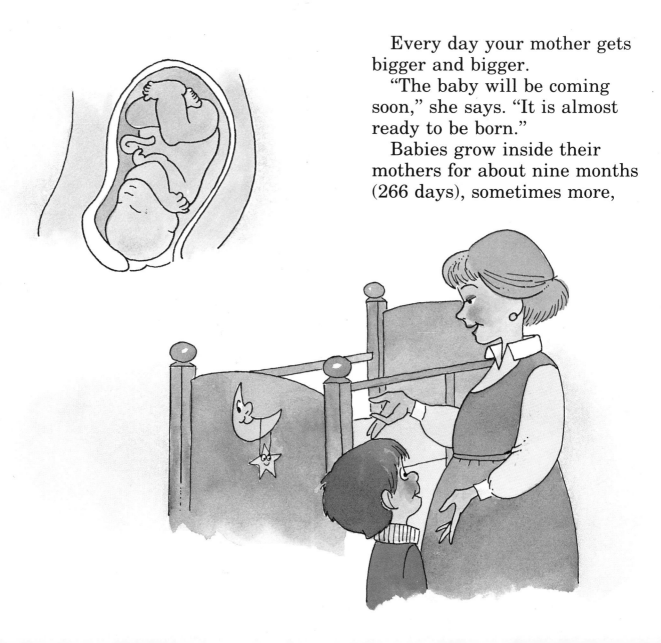

Every day your mother gets bigger and bigger.

"The baby will be coming soon," she says. "It is almost ready to be born."

Babies grow inside their mothers for about nine months (266 days), sometimes more,

e born?

sometimes less. That is a long time. But babies need that time to grow and develop so that they can be strong and healthy.

In that time, the baby will grow to almost 60 cm long and will weigh 2.7 to 4 kg, more or less. Then baby is ready.

No one knows exactly when the baby will come, even the doctor doesn't know for sure. Everyone wonders: "Is it a boy or a girl?" "How much will it weigh?" "Will it have hair or be bald?" And, most of all: "When will the baby be born?"

"HELLO!" (hello) "I'M HERE!" (I'm here)

Have you ever shouted and heard your voice echo back to you?

When you talk, invisible sound waves travel away from your mouth and go through the air. People can hear what you say when the sound waves go in their ears.

If a wall or mountain or canyon is in front of you when you talk loudly, your sound waves go out and are *reflected* or bounced right back to you! Then

an echo?

you hear what you just said repeated again in an echo. Sometimes you can hear the echo again and again as the sound waves bounce off many places.

Try standing ten or more metres away from a large, flat wall. Speak loudly and listen for your echo. Your sound waves are bouncing back to you! That's when you can hear an echo!

When does a volcanc

A volcano is an opening in the earth. The opening goes down many miles under the ground to where the earth is so hot that rock there is melted. This melted rock is called magma.

The pressure under the ground may become too great from the weight of the heavy rock pressing on the magma. Then the volcano erupts. Red-hot magma blasts up through the opening in the surface of the earth and pours out onto the ground. Then it is called lava.

erupt?

Hot ashes, rocks, dust, and gas shoot up into the air. Sometimes many people are hurt or killed and much land is destroyed.

Scientists cannot tell exactly when a volcano will erupt. But they often see warning signs. The ground shakes and steam comes out of the top of the volcano. Scientists use special machines to measure the pressure of the magma underground. They can warn people to go far away from a volcano when it is about to erupt.

Your half-birthday is the day that is halfway between your last birthday and your birthday the next year. On your half-birthday, you officially become 5½ or 7½ or 10½ or whatever.

Here is how you can figure out your half-birthday. Think of the month and day of your birthday. Count six months (which is half a year) *past* your birthday month. The day will

s my half-birthday?

stay the same. The new date you get is your half-birthday.

If your birthday is May 15, then your half-birthday is six months later, on November 15. If your birthday is July 22, then your half-birthday is January 22.

On your half-birthday, you will know that you are a half-year older. Maybe you can plan to celebrate your half-birthday by having a party!

When will an acorn grow

It is hard to believe that a small acorn can grow into a tall oak tree. But it does! This does not happen quickly, though. Just like a person, a tree needs time to grow up.

Inside an acorn there is a big seed — and food to feed it as it begins to grow.

Acorns fall down to the ground in autumn. In spring, the seeds begin to sprout. Rain and sunshine and soil help the seeds grow into oak trees. The

ɔ be a tall tree?

trees grow slowly. By the end of the first year, they may be only 60 to 90 centimetres high.

Each year, the oak trees grow taller. After about 25 years, they are 18 metres tall!

If you plant an acorn when you are a small child, the acorn will have grown into a tall tree when you have grown into an adult!

lo baby robins fly?

When baby robins first hatch from their eggs, they are very weak and tiny. And they are hungry!

Mother and father robins search all day to find worms and insects to feed their hungry babies.

Each day, the baby robins grow bigger and stronger. They also grow their first coat of feathers.

When the baby birds are about two weeks old, they begin to try to fly. At first it is hard work, and they can only flutter for a short distance. But soon, they are gliding through the air and finding their own food just like their parents.

When can I skate

When winter comes, it is a lot of fun to go ice skating on a frozen pond.

But before you skate, always check to see if the ice is strong enough to hold you up safely. Ice on a pond needs to be 15

n the pond?

centimetres thick to support a group of ice skaters. If the ice is not that thick, the weight of the people may make the ice crack and cause a dangerous accident.

Often you will see a flag posted next to a pond to tell whether or not it is safe for ice skating. A white flag is a sign for a safe pond. But a red flag means "Stay away. This pond is not safe for skating."

When were rolle

More than 200 years ago, in Belgium, a man named Joseph Merlin made the first pair of roller skates. He built wooden wheels onto a frame. Next he strapped the frame onto the soles of his shoes. Then, it is said, Mr Merlin rolled into a ballroom on his new skates, while playing a violin — to the great surprise of all the guests!

In 1863, James Plimpton of New York designed a new four-wheeler type of skate. The skates that people use today are like those.

Do you like to roller skate?

kates invented?

When will I know the answers to everything?

You already know many things. And you are always learning new information. Every time you talk to a friend, read a book, take a trip or play a game, you are learning something new.

As you grow older, you may learn how to multiply fractions, paint with oil paints, drive a

car, plant a garden, play chess, and swim the backstroke. And you will learn many, many other things, too.

But you will never know the answers to everything. No one ever will. There will always be new things to learn and discover. And that is one of the wonderful things about life.